The Silly Little Book of CLASSROOM JOKES

The Silly Little Book of

CLASSROOM JOKES

This is a Parragon Book

This edition published in 2002

Parragon
Queen Street House
4 Queen Street
Bath BA1 1HE, UK

Produced by Magpie Books an imprint of
Robinson Publishing Ltd, London

Hardback ISBN 0-75258-624-6
Paperback ISBN 0-75258-632-7

A copy of the British Library Cataloguing-in-Publication Data is available from the British Library

Printed and bound in China

Contents

MAD MATH 1

IN THE LAB 17

MUSICAL MAYHEM 26

GENERAL STUDIES 39

CLASSROOM CAPERS 60

QUESTIONS AND ANSWERS 95

SICKIES 125

TEACHER'S PESTS 143

PROUD PARENTS 171

DINNERTIME 203

EXAMS AND REPORTS 220

SCHOOL'S OUT 235

Introduction

Instead of falling asleep at your desk, why not surprise and amuse your classmates by informing everyone that the coldest place in the world is Chile, that geese like to eat gooseberries, that Lake Eerie is full of ghosts and that rulers are for measuring how long you can sleep! If you're lucky, you might find yourself the new teacher's pet – locked up in a cage in the corner!

Mad Math

A blind rabbit and a blind snake ran into each other on the road one day. The snake reached out, touched the rabbit and said, "You're soft and fuzzy and have floppy ears. You must be a rabbit." The rabbit reached out, touched the snake and said "You're slimy, beady-eyed and low to the ground. You must be a math teacher."

Two schoolboys were talking about their math lessons. "Why do you suppose we stop the tables at

twelve?" asked one.
"Oh, don't you know," said the other. "I heard Mom say it was unlucky to have thirteen at table."

Did you hear about the math teacher who fainted in class?
Everyone tried to bring her 2.

Why did the math teacher take a ruler to bed with him?
He wanted to see how long he would sleep.

What's the longest piece of furniture in the school?
The multiplication table.

Teacher: What's the best way to pass this geometry test?
Boy: Knowing all the angles.

"The girl beside me in math is very clever," said Alec to his mother. "She has enough brain for two."
"Perhaps you'd better think of marriage," replied Mom.

"Frank," said the weary math teacher, "if you had seven dollars in your pocket, and seven dollars in another pocket, what would you have?"
"Someone else's trousers on!"

In the summer vacation the math teacher collected information for a national opinion poll. But after a week she was sacked. Her vital statistics were wrong.

The math teacher and the English teacher went out for a quick pizza after school. "How long will the pizzas be?" asked the math teacher.

"Sorry, Sir," replied the waiter, "we don't do long pizzas, just ordinary round ones."

Did you hear about the boy who had a soft spot for his math teacher?

It was a bog in the middle of Ireland.

Clarrie: Our math teacher has long black hair all down her back.
Barry: Yes, it's a pity it doesn't grow on her head.

Teacher: Recite your tables to me, Joan.
Joan: Dining table, kitchen table, bedside table . . .

Dad: What did you learn in school today, son?
Son: I learned that those sums you did for me were wrong!

Father: I want to take my girl out of this terrible math class.
Teacher: But she's top of the class.
Father: That's why I think it must be terrible.

Girl: Mom, you know you're always worried about me failing math?
Mother: Yes.
Girl: Well, your worries are over.

Mother: Do you know a girl named Jenny Simon?
Daughter: Yes, she sleeps next to me in math.

Did you hear about the schoolboy who just couldn't get to grips with decimals?
He couldn't see the point.

Tom: Why are you scratching your head?
Harry: I have those arithmetic bugs again.
Tom: Arithmetic bugs – what are they?
Harry: Well, some people call them head lice.
Tom: Then why do you call them arithmetic bugs?

Harry: Because they add to my misery, subtract from my pleasure, divide my attention and multiply like crazy!

What did the arithmetic book say to the geometry book?
Boy! Do we have our problems!

Teacher: If I had ten flies on my desk, and I swatted one, how many flies would be left?
Girl: One – the dead one!

Teacher: Were you copying his sums?
Girl: No, Sir. I was just looking to see if he's got his right.

Mother: Samantha! You came bottom out of ten in arithmetic!
Samantha: Yes, Mom, but it could have been worse.
Mother: How?
Samantha: I could have been in Sarah's group and come bottom out of twenty.

Teacher: Are you good at arithmetic?

Mary: Well, yes and no.

Teacher: What do you mean, yes and no?

Mary: Yes, I'm no good at arithmetic.

Why did some snakes disobey Noah when he told them to "go forth and multiply"?

They couldn't – they were adders.

Teacher: Now, Harrison, if your father borrows $10 from me and pays me back at $1 a month, at the end of six months how much will he owe me?

Harrison: $10, Sir.

Teacher: I'm afraid you don't know much about arithmetic, Harrison.

Harrison: I'm afraid you don't know much about my father!

"Ann!" the teacher shouted one day at the girl who had been daydreaming. "If India has the world's second largest population, oranges are 50 cents for six, and it costs $3 for a day return to Austin, how old am I?"

"32!"

"Why did you say that?"

"Well, my brother's 16 and he's half mad!"

Teacher: If you add 20,567 to 23,678 and then divide by 97 what do you get?

Jim: The wrong answer.

A farmer was showing a schoolboy round his farm when they came to a field where the farmer's sheep were grazing. "How many sheep do you reckon there are?" the farmer asked proudly.

"Seven hundred and sixty-four," replied the boy after a few seconds.

The farmer gaped. "That's exactly right, boy. How did you count them so quickly?"

"Simple, said the boy genius. "I just counted the legs and divided by four!"

In The Lab

Mr Anderson, the science teacher, was very absent-minded. One day he brought a box into the classroom and said, "I've got a frog and a toad in here. When I get them out we'll look at the differences." He put his hand into the box and pulled out two ham sandwiches. "Oh dear!" he said. "I could have sworn I'd just had my lunch."

"What are the elements, Alec?" asked the science teacher.
"Er . . . earth . . . air . . . fire . . ."

"Well done," said the teacher. "There's one more."

"Er . . . oh yes. Golf."

"Golf!"

"Yes, I heard my mom say that dad's in his element when he plays golf."

Mouse One: I've trained that crazy science teacher at last.

Mouse Two: How have you done that?

Mouse One: I don't know how, but every time I run through that maze and ring the bell, he gives me a piece of cheese.

"Now remember boys and girls," said the science teacher. "You can tell a tree's age by counting the rings in a cross- section. One ring for each year."
Alec went home for tea and found a Swiss roll on the table. "I'm not eating that, Mom," he said. "It's five years old."

Science teacher: What happened when electricity was first discovered?
Alex: Someone got a nasty shock.

Why did the science teacher marry the school cleaner?
Because he swept her off her feet.

"Now don't forget boys," the science teacher droned on. "If it wasn't for water we would never learn to swim. And if we'd never learned to swim, just think how many people would have drowned!"

"Philip," asked the chemistry teacher, "what is HNO_3?"

"Oh, er . . . just a minute, Miss, er . . . it's on the tip of my tongue . . ."

"Well in that case – spit it out. It's nitric acid!"

Science Teacher: Can you tell me one substance that conducts electricity, Jane?
Jane: Why, er . . .
Science Teacher: Wire is correct.

Mrs Turbot, the biology teacher, was very fond of fish. She was also rather deaf, which was great for the children in her class. "What Mrs Turbot needs," said one of her colleagues, "is a herring aid."

What's the most important thing to remember in Chemistry?
Never lick the spoon.

Baby Skunk: But, Mom, why can't I have a chemistry set for my birthday?
Mother: Because it would stink the house out, that's why.

Biology Teacher: What kinds of birds do we get in captivity?
Janet: Jail birds, Miss!

Thinking he would play a trick on the biology teacher, Alec glued a beetle's head to a caterpillar's body and very carefully attached some butterfly wings, ant's legs and a fly's tail. The teacher was very impressed. "I've never seen anything like this, Alec," he said. "Tell me, did it hum when you caught it?"

"Why yes, Sir. Quite loudly."

"I thought so. It's a humbug."

Musical Mayhem

Why was the music teacher arrested?
For getting into treble.

Henry: I'd like to learn to play a drum, Sir.
Music Teacher: Beat it!

What is wet and slippery and likes Latin American music?
A conga eel.

What kind of musical instrument do rats play?
Mouse organ.

Why did the singing teacher have such a high pitched voice?
She had falsetto teeth.

How do you know if a monster is musical?
He's got a flat head.

What do you call a musical insect?
A humbug.

Why did the school orchestra have bad manners?
Because it didn't know how to conduct itself.

Why is a pupil learning to sing like someone opening a tin of sardines?
Because they both have trouble with the key.

What is the difference between a musician and a dead witch?
One composes and the other decomposes.

What is the witches' favorite musical?
My Fear Lady.

What do ghosts dance to?
Soul music.

The music teacher could not control her class. A deafening noise always came from her room. One day when it was worse than usual the English teacher could bear it no longer. She ran into the music room where she found the music teacher sitting at her piano and the boys and girl raising Cain.

"Do you know my pupils can't concentrate for the din in here?" the English teacher said.

"No!" said the music teacher. "But if you hum it I'll try and follow."

How do ghosts learn songs?
They read the sheet music.

Did you hear about the musical ghost?
He wrote haunting melodies.

Why don't skeletons play music in church?
They have no organs.

Modern music isn't as bad as it sounds.

Music Student: Did you really learn to play the violin in six easy lessons?
Music Teacher: Yes, but the 500 that followed were pretty difficult.

Bob: Our teacher is very musical you know.
Ben: Musical? Mr.Jenkinson?
Bob: Yes. He's always fiddling with his beard.

Piano Tuner: I've come to tune the piano.
Music Teacher: But we didn't send for you.
Piano Tuner: No, but the people who live across the street did.

Why did Ken keep his trumpet in the fridge?
Because he liked cool music.

At my piano teacher's last performance the audience cheered and cheered. The piano was locked!

What's a skeleton's favorite musical instrument?
A trombone.

What does the music teacher do when he's locked out of the classroom?
Sing until he gets the right key.

What kind of piano music do witches like best?
Hagtime.

Why did the music student have a piano in the bathroom?
Because he was practicing Handel's Water Music.

Why did the music teacher spend all his time in bed?
He composed sheet music.

Music Teacher: Do you like opera, Francesca?
Francesca: Apart from the singing, yes.

When is the water in the shower room musical?
When it's piping hot.

What kind of musical instrument can you use for fishing?
The cast-a-net.

Music Teacher: Brian, if f means forte, what does ff mean?
Brian: Eighty!

Teacher: Anyone here quick at picking up music?
Terence and Tony: I am, Sir!
Teacher: Right, you two. Move that piano!

General Studies

Found in the school library: *The Broken Window* by Eva Brick

When is a blue school book not a blue school book?
When it is read.

Did you hear about the brilliant geography master?
He had abroad knowledge of his subject.

Teacher: What's this a picture of?
Class: Don't know, Miss.
Teacher: It's a kangaroo.
Class: What's a kangaroo, Miss?
Teacher: A kangaroo is a native of Australia.
Smallest Boy: Wow, my sister's married one of them!

Geography Teacher: What mineral do we import from America?
Dumb Darren: Coca Cola!

Geography Teacher: Matthew, what is the climate of New Zealand?
Matthew: Very cold, Sir.
Geography Teacher: Wrong.
Matthew: But, Sir! When they send us meat, it always arrives frozen!

On her vacation, the geography teacher explained to the history teacher that she went to the Himalayas, visiting remote mountain areas. In fact, she said, we went where the hand of man had never set foot.

Simple Simon was writing a geography essay. It began: "The people who live in Paris are called parasites . . ."

"Who was Captain Kidd?" asked the history teacher.
"He was a contortionist."
"What makes you think that, Alec?"
"Well it says in the history book that he spent a lot of time sitting on his chest."

Geography teacher: What is the coldest place in the world?
Ann: Chile.

"Can anyone think of a vegetable that's mentioned in the Bible?" asked the English teacher.
"Lettuce, Sir," said Alec.
"I don't think so, Alec," the teacher said.
"Oh yes, Sir," protested Alec. "Someone says, Lettuce with a gladsome mind praise the Lord for he is kind."

Teacher: Barbara, name three collective nouns.
Barbara: The wastepaper bin, the trash can and the vacuum cleaner.

"That's an excellent essay for someone your age," said the English teacher.
"How about for someone my Mom's age, Miss?"

An English teacher asked her class to write an essay on what they'd do if they had $1,000,000. Alec handed in a blank sheet of paper.

"Alec!" yelled the teacher. "You've done nothing. Why?"

"'Cos if I had $1,000,000 that's exactly what I would do."

What do you call an English teacher, five feet tall, covered from head to toe in boils and totally bald?

Sir!

"Why have you written that Shakespeare was a corset manufacturer before he became a playwright?" asked the English teacher.
"Because he wrote that he could put a girdle round the earth in forty minutes."

When is an English teacher like a judge?
When she hands out long sentences.

"Alec," said the religious education teacher, "you've written here that Samson was an actor. What makes you think that?"

"Well, Sir," said Alec, "I read that he brought the house down."

I wouldn't say our English teacher is fat, but when she got on a Speak Your Weight machine it surrendered.

English Teacher: Now give me a sentence using the word "fascinate."
Clara: My raincoat has ten buttons but I can only fasten eight.

Why is history like a fruit cake?
Because it's full of dates.

Phil: Who was the fastest runner in history?
Bill: Adam. He was first in the human race.

What's your handicrafts teacher like?
She's a sew and sew.

Boy to Friend: My dad is so old, when he was in school, history was called current events.

Barbara: I wish I'd been alive a few hundred years ago.
History teacher: Why?
Barbara: There'd have been a lot less history to learn.

Art Teacher: What color would you paint the sun and the wind?
Brian: The sun rose, and the wind blue.

Monica fancied herself as an artist. But her art teacher said she was so bad it was a wonder she could draw breath.

The cookery teacher was in a delicatessen buying nuts for the afternoon's cake baking. "What kind of nuts would you like?" asked the salesclerk.

"Cashew," replied the teacher.

"Bless you," said the salesclerk. "What kind of nuts would you like?"

"Well, children," said the cannibal cookery teacher. "What did you make of the new English teacher?"

"Burgers, Miss."

Typing Teacher: Bob! Your work has certainly improved. There are only ten mistakes here.

Bob: Oh good, Miss.

Teacher: Now let's look at the second line, shall we?

Do you know that if you laid all the economics teachers in the world end to end you'd still not come to a definite conclusion?

Our favorite teacher, Miss Rockey
Wanted to train as a jockey.
But, sad to recall,
She grew far too tall.
So now she teaches us field
hockey.

The physical education mistress had broken off her engagement. The science mistress asked her what had happened. "I thought it was love at first sight," said the science mistress.

"It was, but it was the second and third sights that changed my mind."

Why did the idiots' tug o' war team lose the match?
They pushed.

Teacher: Write "I must not forget my gym kit" 100 times.
Nicky: But, Sir, I only forgot it once.

Why did the insects drop the centipede from their soccer team?
It took him so long to put his boots on.

What's the difference between a gymnastics teacher and a duck?
One goes quick on its legs, the other goes quack on its legs.

May: What position does your brother play in the school soccer team?

Jay: I think he's one of the drawbacks.

A gym teacher who came from Quebec,
Wrapped both legs around his neck.
But sad, he forgot
How to untie the knot.
And now he's a highly strung wreck.

Dickie: I hear the school baseball team's prospects are looking up.
Nicky: Oh good, are you leaving it then?

Bob had just missed a shot at goal, which meant the other team won. "I could kick myself," he groaned, as the players came off the pitch.
"Don't bother," said the captain, "you'd miss."

"Lie flat on your backs, class, and circle your feet in the air as if you were riding your bikes," said the gym teacher.

"Alec! What are you doing. Move your feet, boy."

"I'm freewheeling, Sir."

Classroom Capers

Two teenage boys were talking in the classroom. One said, "I took my girlfriend to see *The Bride of Dracula* last night."

"Oh yeah," said the other, "what was she like?"

"Well she was about six foot six, white as a ghost and she had big red staring eyes and fangs."

The other said, "Yes, but what was *The Bride of Dracula* like?"

Teacher to pupil: How many thousand times have I told you not to exaggerate?

Why was the big, hairy, two-headed monster top of the class in school?
Because two heads are better than one.

Did you hear about the teacher whose pupils were so studious that when she walked into the classroom and said good morning they wrote it in their notebooks?

When the school was broken into, the thieves took absolutely everything – desks, books, blackboards, everything apart from the soap in the lavatories and all the towels. The police are looking for a pair of dirty criminals.

It was sweltering hot outside. The teacher came into the classroom wiping his brow and said, "Ninety-two today. Ninety-two."

"Happy birthday to you. Happy birthday to you . . ." sang the class.

Anna: I was top of the class last week.

Mom: How did you manage that?

Anna: I managed to answer a question about elephants.

Mom: What question?

Anna: Well, the teacher asked us how many legs an elephant had, and I said five.

Mom: But that wasn't right.

Anna: I know, but it was the nearest anyone got.

"Why don't you like this country?" the teacher asked a Californian boy who had come to an English school.
"It's the weather," drawled Bud. "I'm not used to the rain. Back home we have 365 days of sunshine every year – at least."

Sign outside the school caretaker's hut: Will the person who took my ladder please return it, or further steps will be taken.

"What's your father's occupation?" asked the school secretary on the first day of the new term.

"He's a conjurer, Miss," said the new boy.

"How interesting. What's his favorite trick?"

"He saws people in half."

"Golly! Now next question. Any brothers and sisters?"

"One half brother and two half sisters."

On the first day in school the children were sizing each other up and boasting, trying to make good impressions on each other.

"I come from a one-parent family," said one little girl proudly.

"That's nothing," said another. "Both my parents remarried after they got divorced. I came from a four-parent family."

Why did the school cleaner take early retirement?

Because he realized that grime doesn't pay.

Teacher: Fred! Wipe that mud off your shoes before you come in the classroom.
Fred: But, Sir, I'm not wearing any shoes.

"I hope you're not one of those boys who sits and watches the school clock," said the principal to a new boy.
"No, Sir. I've got a digital watch that bleeps at half past three."

"Your daughter's only five and she can spell her name backward? Why that is remarkable." The principal was talking to a parent who was trying to impress her with the child's academic prowess so that she would be accepted into the school.

"Yes, we're very proud of her," said the mother.

"And what is your daughter's name?"

"Anna."

Miss Simons agreed to be interviewed by Alec for the school magazine. "How old are you, Miss?" asked Alec.

"I'm not going to tell you that."

"But Mr Hill the technical teacher and Mr Hill the geography teacher told me how old they were."

"Oh well," said Miss Simons. "I'm the same age as both of them."

The poor teacher was not happy when she saw what Alec wrote: "Miss Simons, our English teacher, confided in me that she was as old as the Hills."

"I did not come into the classroom to listen to you lot being impertinent," complained the teacher.
"Oh! Where do you usually go, Miss?"

A little firefly was in school one day and he put up his hand. "Please, Miss, may I be excused?"
"Yes," replied the teacher, "when you've got to glow, you've got to glow."

"Why are you crying Alec?" asked the teacher.

"'Cos my parrot died last night. I washed it in soap powder . . ."

"Alec," said the teacher. "You must have known that soap powder's bad for parrots."

"Oh it wasn't the soap powder that killed it, Sir. It was the spin drier."

Carol: Our teacher gives me the pip.

Darryl: What's her name?

Carol: Miss Lemmon.

Teacher: I see you don't cut your hair any longer.
Nigel: No, Sir, I cut it shorter.

"Where's your pencil, Bud?" the teacher asked an American boy who had just come to school.
"I ain't got one, Sir."
"You're in England now, Bud. Not ain't, haven't. I haven't got a pencil. You haven't got a pencil. They haven't got a pencil."
"Gee!" said Bud. "Pop said things were tough in this country, but I didn't know pencils were so hard to come by."

Little Tommy was the quietest boy in school. He never answered any questions but his homework was always excellent. If anyone said anything to him he would simply nod, or shake his head. The staff thought he was shy and decided to do something to give him confidence. "Tommy," said his teacher. "I've just bet Miss Smith $5 I can get you to say three words. You can have half." Tommy looked at her pityingly and said, "You lose."

"Please, Miss!" said a little boy at kindergarten. "We're going to play elephants and circuses, do you want to join in?"

"I'd love to," said the teacher. "What do you want me to do?"

"You can be the lady that feeds us peanuts!"

"Why are you crying Amanda?" asked her teacher.

"'Cos Jenny's broken my new doll, Miss," she cried.

"How did she do that?"

"I hit her on the head with it."

A mother was desperate to get her under-age daughter into kindergarten and was trying to impress the principal with the child's intellectual abilities. "She'll easily keep up with the others even though she is a year younger."

"Well," said the teacher doubtfully. "Could she prove it by saying something?"

"Certainly, Miss," said the child. "Something pertaining to your conversation or something purely irrelevant?"

"What's your first name?" the teacher asked a new boy.
"It's Orson, Miss. I was named after Orson Welles, the film star."
"Just as well your last name's not Cart."
"No, Miss, it's Trapp."

Did you know that eight out of every ten schoolchildren use ballpoint pens to write with? Gosh! What do the other two use them for?

Teacher: Dennis! When you yawn you should put your hand to your mouth.
Dennis: What, and get it bitten?

There was once a lad called Willy Maufe. When he went to school for the first time the teacher asked him his name. "I'm Maufe," said Willy.
"Don't be silly, boy," said the teacher. "You'll stay here till 3.30 like the rest of us."

The teacher glanced up at the clock and then checked the time with his watch. "That clock's fast," he told the class.

"I hope so, Sir. If it isn't, it'll fall down and break."

Teacher: You're wearing a very strange pair of socks, Darren. One's blue with red spots, and one's yellow with green stripes.

Darren: Yes, and I've got another pair just the same at home.

Mandy: Our teacher went on a special banana diet.
Andy: Did she lose weight?
Mandy: No, but she couldn't half climb trees well!

Teacher: You weren't in school last Friday, Robert. I heard you were out playing baseball.

Robert: That's not true, Sir. And I've got the movie tickets to prove it.

Dave: The trouble with our teachers is that they all do bird impressions.

Mave: Really? What do they do?

Dave: They watch us like hawks.

Andy: What's the difference between a wage and a salary, Miss?

Teacher: If you earn a wage, you are paid every week, if you earn a salary, you are paid every month. Teachers, for example, get paid salaries because they are paid monthly.

Andy: Please, Miss, where do they work?

Sign on the school noticeboard: Guitar for sale, cheap, no strings attached.

Teacher: Martin, put some more water in the fish tank.
Martin: But, Sir, they haven't drunk the water I gave them yesterday.

Did you hear about the teacher who was trying to instill good table manners in her girls?
She told them, "A well mannered girl never crumbles her bread or rolls in her soup."

Rob: I must rush home and cut the lawn.
Teacher: Did your father promise you something if you cut it?
Rob: No, he promised me something if didn't!

Teacher: Andrew, your homework looks as if it is in your father's handwriting.
Andrew: Well, I used his pen, Sir.

Keith: Our teacher's an old bat.
Kevin: You mean he's bad tempered?
Keith: Not only that, he hangs around us all the time.

Two teachers were reminiscing about their deprived childhood. "I lived in a tough neighborhood," said the first. "People were afraid to walk the streets after dark."
"That's nothing," said the other, "whenever I hung my Christmas stocking up by the fireplace, Santa Claus stole it."

Wife to Husband: I think Spencer may grow up to be a space scientist. I was talking to his teacher today and she said he was taking up space.

Arthur: It's true that there is a connection between television and violence.

Martha: What makes you think that?

Arthur: Because I told my teacher I had watched television instead of doing my homework, and she hit me.

Harry: Please may I have another pear, Miss?
Teacher: Another, Harry? They don't grow on trees, you know.

Teacher: Are you really going to leave school, Ben, or are you just saying that to brighten my day?

Casper: I was the teacher's pet last year.
Jasper: Why was that?
Casper: She couldn't afford a dog.

Ben's teacher regards him as a wonder child.
He wonders whether Ben will ever learn anything.

Teacher: Didn't you know the bell had gone?
Silly Sue: I didn't take it, Miss.

Teacher: I'd like to go through one whole day without having to punish you.
Girl: You have my permission, Sir.

Teacher: Colin, one of your essays is very good but the other one I can't read.
Colin: Yes, Sir. My mother is a much better writer than my father.

Teacher: I told you to write this poem out twenty times because your handwriting is so bad.
Girl: I'm sorry, Miss – my arithmetic's not that good either.

Teacher: You should have been here at nine o'clock.
Boy: Why? Did something happen?

Teacher: I wish you'd pay a little attention.
Girl: I'm paying as little as possible.

One unfortunate teacher started off a lesson with the following instruction: "I want you all to give me a list of the lower animals, starting with Georgina Clark . . ."

Teacher: Tommy Russell, you're late again.
Tommy: Sorry, Sir. It's my bus – it's always coming late.
Teacher: Well, if it's late again tomorrow, catch an earlier one.

"Sir!" said Alexander. "Empty Coke cans, old food wrappers, plastic bags, used tissues, broken bottles, empty boxes . . ."
"Alexander!" snapped the teacher. "You're talking garbage again!"

Teacher: Mason, what is the outer part of a tree called?
Mason: Don't know, Sir.
Teacher: Bark, boy, bark!
Mason: Woof-woof!

"How old would you say I am, Francis?" the teacher asked.
"Forty, Sir," said the boy promptly.
"You seem very sure," said the puzzled teacher. "What makes you think I'm forty?"
"My big brother's twenty, Sir," replied the boy, "and you're twice as dumb as he is!"

Teacher: Martin, I've taught you everything I know, and you're still ignorant!

"Melanie," said the teacher sharply, "you've been doing Rebecca's homework for her again! I recognized your writing in her exercise book."

"I haven't, Miss," declared Melanie. "It's just that we use the same pencil!"

A class of five-year-olds had been told to draw a scene representing the flight into Egypt.
One little tot proudly displayed a drawing of a jumbo jet containing the three members of the Holy Family – but also a fourth figure.
"When I said 'flight,' I didn't quite mean a jet plane," said the teacher. "However, we'll let that pass for now. But who is the fourth person on the plane?"
To which the little one replied, "That's Pontius Pilate."

Questions and Answers

Confucius he say: If teacher ask you question and you not know answer, mumble.

Why is a classroom like an old car? Because it's full of nuts, and has a crank at the front.

Teacher: If you saw me standing by a witch, what fruit would it remind you of?
Pupil: A pear.

What is the most popular sentence at school?
I don't know.

"Why are you tearing up your homework notebook and scattering the pieces around the classroom?" a furious teacher asked one of her pupils.
"To keep the elephants away, Miss."
"There are no elephants."
"Shows how effective it is then, doesn't it?"

What do you get if you cross a caretaker with an elephant?
A twenty-ton school cleaner.

Why is school like a shower?
One wrong turn and you're in hot water.

Teacher: What did Robert the Bruce do after watching the spider climbing up and down?
Pupil: He invented the yo-yo.

Teacher: Have you ever seen a duchess?
Pupil: Yes – it's the same as an English "s"!

Knock, knock.
Who's there?
Quiet Tina.
Quiet Tina who?
Quiet Tina classroom.

Did you hear about the posh school where all the pupils smelled?
It was for filthy rich kids only.

What are pupils at ghost schools called?
Ghoulboys and ghoulgirls.

What did the ghost teacher say to her class?
Watch the board and I'll go through it again.

"Mary," said her teacher, "you can't bring that lamb into school. What about the smell?"
"Oh, that's all right, Miss," said Mary. "It'll soon get used to it."

A school inspector was talking to a pupil. "How many teachers work in this school?" he asked.
"Only about half of them, I reckon," replied the pupil.

Why should a school not be near a chicken farm?
To avoid the pupils overhearing fowl language.

Kelly: Is God a doctor, Miss?
Teacher: In some ways, Kelly. Why do you ask?
Kelly: Because the Bible says that the Lord gave the tablets to Moses.

"What were you before you came to school, boys and girls?" asked the teacher, hoping that someone would say "Babies."
She was disappointed when all the children cried out "Happy!"

Knock, knock.
Who's there?
Teacher.
Teacher who?
Teacher-self French.

Teacher: I was going to read you a story called *The Invasion of the Body Snatchers*, but I've changed my mind.

Class: Oh why, Miss?

Teacher: Because we might get carried away.

Teacher: Who can tell me what "dogma" means?

Cheeky Charlie: It's a lady dog that's had puppies, Sir.

"Welcome to school, Simon," said the nursery school teacher to the new boy. "How old are you?"

"I'm not old," said Simon. "I'm nearly new."

"Please, Miss! How do you spell ichael?"

The teacher was rather bewildered. "Don't you mean Michael?"

"No, Miss. I've written the 'M' already."

Why are teachers jealous of driving instructors?
Because driving instructors are allowed to belt their pupils.

The teacher was furious with her son. "Just because you've been put in my class, there's no need to think you can take liberties. You're a pig."
The boy said nothing. "Well! Do you know what a pig is?"
"Yes, Mom," said the boy. "The offspring of a swine."

"Please, Sir! Please, Sir! Why do you keep me locked up in this cage?"
"Because you're the teacher's pet."

The school teacher was furious when Alec knocked him down with his new bicycle in the playground. "Don't you know how to ride that yet?" he roared.
"Oh yes!" shouted Alec over his shoulder. "It's the bell I can't work yet."

Chuck: Do you have holes in your underpants?
Teacher: No, of course not.
Chuck: Then how do you get your feet through?

Teacher: And did you see the Catskill Mountains on your trip to America?
Jimmy: No, but I saw them kill mice.

Teacher: Who can tell me what geese eat?

Paul: Er, gooseberries, Sir?

Teacher: What is the longest night of the year?

Alex: A fortnight.

Teacher: What's the difference between a buffalo and a bison?
Student: You can't wash your hands in a buffalo, Miss.

Tracy: Would you punish someone for something they haven't done?
Teacher: Of course not.
Tracy: Oh good, because I haven't done my homework.

Retired colonel, talking of the good old days: Have you ever hunted bear?
His grandson's teacher: No, but I've been fishing in shorts.

Teacher: What do you know about Lake Erie?
Rose: It's full of ghosts, Miss.

Teacher: And why would you like to be a teacher, Clarence?
Clarence: Because I wouldn't have to learn anything, Sir. I'd know everything by then.

Teacher: Name six things that contain milk.
Dumb Dora: Custard, cocoa, and four cows.

Teacher: Peter! Why are you scratching yourself?
Peter: 'Cos no one else knows where I itch.

Teacher: Who can tell me what an archeologist is?
Tracey: It's someone whose career is in ruins.

Teacher: Why are you late, Penelope?
Penelope: I was obeying the sign that says "Children – Dead Slow," Miss.

Teacher: Who knows what a hippy is?
Clever Dick: It's something that holds your leggy on.

Did you hear about the boy who was told to do 100 lines?
He drew 100 cats on the paper. He thought the teacher had said lions.

Teacher: What's a robin?
John: A bird that steals, Miss.

Teacher: Can anyone tell me what a shamrock is?
Jimmy: It's a fake diamond, Miss.

Teacher: Who can tell me where Turkey is?
Dumb Donald: We ate ours last Christmas, Miss.

Knock, knock.
Who's there?
Alison.
Alison who?
Alison to my teacher!

Teacher: Why are you always late?
Roger: I threw away my alarm clock.
Teacher: But why did you throw away your alarm clock?
Roger: Because it always went off when I was asleep.

Teacher: Why did the Romans build straight roads?
Alex: So the Britons couldn't lie in ambush round the corners.

Teacher: What is meant by "doggerel"?
Terry: Little dogs, Miss.

Teacher: Why do birds fly south in winter?
Jim: Because it's too far to walk.

Boy: Why did you throw my homework in the bin?
Teacher: Because it was trash.

Teacher: Who was the first woman on earth?
Angela: I don't know, Sir.
Teacher: Come on, Angela, it has something to do with an apple.
Angela: Granny Smith?

Teacher: What happened to your homework?
Boy: I made it into a paper plane and someone hijacked it.

Teacher: Why are you standing on your head?
Boy: I'm just trying to turn things over in my mind, Sir.

Teacher: Who can tell me what BC stands for?
Girl: Before calculators.

Girl: Why do you call me pilgrim?
Teacher: Because you're making so little progress.

Teacher: Why did you put that frog in Melinda's case?
Boy: Because I couldn't find a mouse.

Teacher: Billy. Didn't you hear me call you?
Billy: Yes, Miss, but you told us yesterday not to answer back.

Teacher: You seem to be exceedingly ignorant, Williams. Have you read Dickens?

Williams: No, Sir.

Teacher: Have you read Shakespeare?

Williams: No, Sir.

Teacher: Well, what have you read?

Williams: Er . . . er . . . I've red hair, Sir.

Teacher: What is the plural of mouse?
Pupil: Mice.
Teacher: And what is the plural of baby?
Pupil: Twins.

Teacher: Alan, give me a sentence starting with "I."
Alan: I is . . .
Teacher: No, Alan. You must always say "I am."
Alan: Oh right. I am the ninth letter of the alphabet.

Teacher: Spell the word "needle," Kenneth.

Kenneth: N, e, i . . .

Teacher: No, Kenneth, there's no "i" in needle.

Kenneth: Then it's a rotten needle, Miss!

Teacher: Carol, what is "can't" short for?

Carol: Cannot.

Teacher: And what is "don't" short for?

Carol: Doughnut!

Sickies

Nigel: You said the school dentist would be painless, but he wasn't.
Teacher: Did he hurt you?
Nigel: No, but he screamed when I bit his finger.

"I thought, Jessop, that you wanted yesterday afternoon off because you were seeing your dentist?"
"That's right, Sir."
"So how come I saw you and a friend coming out of the football ground at the end of a game?"
"That was my dentist."

What do you give a sick snake?
Asp-rin.

Little Jack's mother was on the telephone to the boy's dentist. "I don't understand it," she complained. "I thought his treatment would only cost me $10, but you've charged me $40."
"It is usually $10, madam," agreed the dentist, "but Jack yelled so loudly that three of my other patients ran away!"

Why is the letter "t" so important to a stick insect?
Without it would be a sick insect.

What can a schoolboy keep and give away at the same time?
A cold.

Why did the class joker go to hospital?
He wanted to learn a few sick jokes.

A schoolboy went home with a pain in his stomach. "Well sit down and eat your supper," said his mother. "Your stomach is hurting because it's empty. It'll be all right when you've got something in it."

Shortly after, Dad came in from the office, complaining of a headache.

"That's because it's empty," said his bright son. "You'd be all right if you had something in it."

School Doctor to Parent: I'm afraid your daughter needs glasses.

Parent: How can you tell?

School Doctor: By the way she came in through the window.

Nurse: How did you manage to get a black eye?

Bertie: You see that tree in the schoolyard?

Nurse: Yes.

Bertie: Well, I didn't.

Where do you take a sick wasp?
To waspital

Did you hear what happened when there was an epidemic of laryngitis at school?
The school nurse sent everyone to the croakroom.

Cannibal Pupil: Nurse, Nurse, I've been eating a missionary and I feel sick.
Nurse: Well, you know what they say – you can't keep a good man down.

"What did the doctor say to you yesterday?" asked the teacher.
"He said I was allergic to horses."
"I've never heard of anyone suffering from that. What's the condition called?"
"Bronco-itis."

Did you hear about the sick werewolf?
He lost his voice but it's howl right now.

"Your pupils must miss you a lot," said the woman in the next bed to the teacher in hospital.
"Not at all! Their aim's usually good. That's why I'm here."

Parent to School Doctor: Will those pills really cure my little Amy?
School Doctor: Well, no one I've given them to has ever come back.

What medicine do you give a sick ant?
Antibiotics.

Why don't anteaters get sick?
Because they're full of anti-bodies!

"Teacher reminds me of the sea," said Alec to Billy.
"You mean she's deep, sometimes calm but occasionally stormy?"
"No! She makes me sick."

What's the best thing to give a seasick elephant?
Plenty of room.

"I suffered from travel sickness on the train this morning," said an absent-minded teacher. "I hate traveling with my back to the engine."
"Why didn't you ask the person in the seat opposite to change with you?" asked his wife.
"I couldn't," said the teacher. "The seat was empty."

What was written on the hypochondriac's tombstone?
I told you I was sick.

School Doctor: Good morning, Jimmy. Haven't seen you for a long time.
Jimmy: I know, doctor. It's because I've been ill.

Statistics say that one in three people is mentally ill. So check your classmates, and if two of them seem OK, you're the one.

Mary arrived home from school covered in spots. "Whatever's the matter?" asked her mother.
"I don't know," replied Mary, "but the teacher thinks I may have caught decimals."

"What do you do?" a young teacher asked the beautiful girl he was dancing with.

"I'm a nurse."

"I wish I could be ill and let you nurse me," he whispered in her ear.

"That would be miraculous. I work on the maternity ward."

What illness did everyone on the Enterprise catch?

Chicken Spocks.

At a very posh boarding school, one of the teachers who was going out for a grand dinner appeared wearing a dinner jacket, evening shirt and black tie. "Oh, Sir," said one of the boys. "You're not wearing those clothes are you? You know they always give you a headache in the morning."

My teacher once stopped a man ill-treating a donkey.
It was a case of brotherly love.

A huge lion was roaring through the jungle when he suddenly saw a tiny mouse. He stopped and snarled at it menacingly. "You're very small," he growled fiercely. "Well, I've been sick," replied the mouse piteously.

Teacher: Ford, you're late for school again. What is it this time?
Ford: I sprained my ankle, Sir.
Teacher: That's a lame excuse.

Billy's mother was called into the school one day by the principal.

"We're very worried about Billy," he said. "He goes round all day clucking."

"That's right," said Billy's mother. "He thinks he's a chicken."

"Haven't you taken him to a psychiatrist?"

"Well we would but we need the eggs."

Teacher's Pests

A pharmacist, a storekeeper and a teacher were sentenced to death by firing squad. The pharmacist was taken from his cell and, as the soldiers took aim, he shouted "Avalanche!" The soldiers panicked and in the confusion the pharmacist escaped. The storekeeper was led out next. As the soldiers took aim he shouted "Flood!" and escaped. The teacher was then led out. The squad took aim and the teacher, remembering how the other two had escaped, shouted "Fire!"

Teachers nowadays specialize so much that they know more and more about less and less until they know everything about nothing!

Why did the teacher have her hair in a bun?
Because she had her nose in a hamburger.

Teacher: I'd like a room, please.
Hotel Receptionist: Single, Sir?
Teacher: Yes, but I am engaged.

Mother: Why do you call your teacher "Treasure"?
Girl: Because we wonder where she was dug up.

Generally speaking, teachers are generally speaking.

"I'm not going to school today," Alexander said to his mother. "The teachers bully me and the boys in my class don't like me."

"You're going. And that's final. I'll give you two good reasons why."

"Why?"

"Firstly, you're 35 years old. Secondly, you're the principal."

Girl: My teacher's a peach.

Mother: You mean she's sweet.

Girl: No, she has a heart of stone.

Why did the teacher wear a life jacket at night?
Because she liked sleeping on a water bed, and couldn't swim!

Knock, knock.
Who's there?
Genoa.
Genoa who?
Genoa good teacher?

A motorist approached the principal one afternoon and said, "I'm awfully sorry, but I think I've just run over the school cat. Can I replace it?"
The principal looked him up and down and replied, "I doubt if you'd be the mouser she was."

What's the difference between a railroad guard and a teacher?
One minds the train, the other trains the mind.

How can a teacher increase the size of her pay check?
By looking at it through a magnifying glass.

What should a teacher take if he's run down?
The number of the car that hit him.

Teacher, in pet shop: I'd like to buy a canary, please. How much do they cost?
Pet shop owner: $10 apiece.
Teacher, horrified: How much does a whole one cost?

Why is a complaining teacher the easiest to satisfy?
Because nothing satisfies them.

What do you get if you cross your least favorite teacher with a telescope?
A horroscope.

Miss Smith and Mrs Brown were having a chat over a cup of tea about why they entered the teaching profession. "I used to be a fortuneteller before I became a teacher," said Miss Smith. "But I had to give it up, there wasn't any future in it."

Why can't the deaf teacher be sent to prison?
Because you can't condemn someone without a hearing.

The young teacher was complaining to her friends about how badly she was being paid. "We get a really poultry amount each month," she said.
"You mean 'paltry'," corrected one of her friends.
"No I don't, I mean 'poultry'," replied the teacher. "What I earn is chicken feed."

A teacher went into a shoe store.
"I'd like some crocodile shoes, please," she said.
"Certainly, Madam," said the salesgirl. "How big is your crocodile?"

What's the difference between a caretaker and a bad-tempered teacher?
Is there any difference?

What's the difference between a schoolteacher and a train?
A schoolteacher says, "Spit out that toffee" and a train says, "Choo, choo."

Did you hear about the teacher who married the dairymaid?
It didn't last. They were like chalk and cheese.

Did you hear about the cross-eyed teacher who had no control over her pupils?

What did the teacher say after spending thousands in the expensive hotel?
I'm sorry to leave, now that I've almost bought the place.

Principal: If you liked your pupils you'd take them to the zoo.
Teacher: Oh, I know some of them come from sub-standard houses, but they can't be that bad, surely.

Why is a man wearing sunglasses like a rotten teacher?
Because he keeps his pupils in the dark.

"You can have that brain there for $5,000," said the brain surgeon to the man who was going to have a brain transplant. "It used to belong to a bank manager. This one's $5,000 too: it was a dancer's. And this one's $50,000: it belonged to a school teacher."

"Why's it ten times more than the others?" gasped the man.

"It's been used ten times less than theirs!"

Why did the Cyclops give up teaching?

Because he only had one pupil.

Why did the teacher decide to become an electrician?
To get a bit of light relief.

I'm not saying our teacher's fat, but every time he falls over he rocks himself to sleep trying to get back up.

How did the teacher knit a suit of armor?
She used steel wool.

"Don't worry, Miss Jones," said the principal to the new teacher. "You'll cope with your new class, but they'll keep you on your toes."
"How's that, Sir?" asked the teacher.
"They always put thumbtacks on the chairs."

Did you hear about the man who took up monster baiting for a living?
He used to be a teacher but he lost his nerve.

Why are teachers happy at Halloween parties?
Because there's lots of school spirit.

"Teacher is a bore!" was scrawled on the blackboard one day. "I do not want to see that on my blackboard," he thundered when he saw it.
"Sorry, Sir! I didn't realize you wanted it kept secret."

What's the difference between teachers and candy?
People like candy.

How did the teacher forecast the weather with a piece of string?
She hung it up, and if it moved, she knew it was windy, and if it got wet, she knew it was raining.

Why did the teacher fix her bed to the chandelier?
Because she was a light sleeper.

Did you hear about the teacher who retired?
His class gave him an illuminated address. They burned his house down.

A teacher was being interviewed for a new job and asked the principal what the hours were. "We try to have early hours you know. I hope that suits."
"Of course," said the teacher. "I don't mind how early I leave."

What's the difference between a boring teacher and a boring book?
You can shut the book up.

The principal was interviewing a new teacher. "You'll get $10,000 to start, with $15,000 after six months."
"Oh!" said the teacher. "I'll come back in six months then."

What is brown, hairy, wears dark glasses and carries a pile of exercise books?
A coconut disguised as a teacher.

"What do you do?" a man asked a very attractive girl at a party.
"I'm an infant teacher."
"Good gracious! I thought you were at least twenty-six."

What do you call a deaf teacher?
Anything you like, he can't hear you.

What do you call a teacher floating on a raft in the sea?
Bob.

Two elderly teachers were talking over old times and saying how much things had changed. "I mean," said the first, "I caught one of the boys kissing one of the girls yesterday."
'Extraordinary," said the second. "I didn't even kiss my wife before I married her, didn't you?"
"I can't remember. What was her maiden name?"

Teacher's strong; teacher's gentle.
Teacher's kind. And I am mental.

Why are art galleries like retirement homes for teachers?
Because they're both full of old masters.

Why did the teacher put corn in his shoes?
Because he had pigeon toes.

What takes a lot of licks from a teacher without complaint?
An ice cream.

How can a teacher double his money?
By folding it in half.

How do teachers dress in mid-January?
Quickly.

Why did the mean teacher walk around with her purse open?
She'd read there was going to be some change in the weather.

Proud Parents

Why was the big, hairy, two-headed monster top of the class in school?
Because two heads are better than one.

What do insects learn in school?
Mothematics.

What school subject are snakes best at?
Hiss-tory.

When Dad came home he was astonished to see Alec sitting on a horse, writing something. "What on earth are you doing there?" he asked.

"Well, teacher told us to write an essay on our favorite animal. That's why I'm here and that's why Susie's sitting in the goldfish bowl!"

What should you do if you find a gorilla sitting at your school desk?
Sit somewhere else.

"Mommy," sobbed the little girl, "I told teacher that great-great grandpapa died at Waterloo, and she said, 'Really, which platform?' and everybody giggled."
"Well next time she says that you just tell her that the platform number is irrelevant."

Mommy, mommy, teacher keeps saying I look like a werewolf.
Be quiet, dear, and go and comb your face.

What do little vampires like to play in school?
Bat's cradle.

What's the favorite subject of young witches in school?
Spelling.

What do little witches do after school?
Their gnomework.

What happened to the naughty little witch at school?
She was ex-spelled.

What is the first thing that vampires learn in school?
The alphabat.

Why do vampires do well in school?
Because every time they're asked a question they come up with a biting reply.

Young Witch: Daddy, I'm so glad you called me Godzilla.
Wizard: Why?
Young Witch: Because that's what the kids call me in school.

First Monster: What is that son of yours doing these days?
Second Monster: He's at medical school.
First Monster: Oh, what's he studying?
Second Monster: Nothing, they're studying him.

Damien was being severely scolded by his father for fighting in school. "Now, Damien," said his angry parent, "this will not do! You must learn that you can't have everything you want in this life. There must always be give and take."

"But there was, Dad!" protested the aggressive youngster. "I gave him a black eye and took the apple."

"Steve, you've been fighting in school again, haven't you?"

"Yes, Mom."

"You must try to control your temper. Didn't I tell you to count to ten?"

"Yes, but Vic's Mom only told him to count up to five, so he hit me first!"

Why is the school swot like quicksand?

Because everything in school sinks into him.

Darren came home from school with two black eyes and a face covered in blood. His mother was horrified. "You've been fighting," she said. "Who did this to you?"

"I don't know his name," replied Darren. "But I'd know him if I met him again. I've got half his left ear in my pocket."

What do you call an ant who honestly hates school?

A tru-ant.

Why didn't the skeleton want to go to school?
Because his heart wasn't in it.

A little boy ran home from school on the first day and pestered his mother into taking him into a toy shop. When they got there he insisted that she buy him a gun.
"But why do you need a gun?" asked his mother . . .
"Because teacher told us she was going to teach us to draw tomorrow."

"It was 'Hamlet'," a boarding school boy wrote to his parents after the school play. "Most of the other boys' parents had seen it before, but they laughed just the same."

Janet came home from school and asked her mother if the aerosol spray in the kitchen was hair lacquer. "No," said Mom. "It's glue."

"I thought so," said Janet. "I wondered why I couldn't get my beret off today."

"Did you thank Mrs Pillbeam for teaching you today?" Alec's mom asked him when he came home from school.

"No I didn't. Mary in front of me did and Mrs Pillbeam said 'Don't mention it' so I didn't."

There once was a schoolboy named Rhett,
Who ate ten Mars Bars for a bet.
When asked Are you faint?
He said, "No I ain't.
But I don't feel like flying a jet."

What's the difference between a schoolboy and an angler?
One baits his hooks. The other hates his books.

Why was the little bird expelled from school?
She was always playing practical yolks.

The principal was very proud of his school's academic record. "It is very impressive," said one parent who was considering sending his son there. "How do you maintain such high standards?"

"Simple," said the principal. "The school motto says it all."

"What's that?" asked the parent.

"If at first you don't succeed, you're expelled."

Teacher: That's the stupidest boy in the whole school.
Mother: That's my son.
Teacher: Oh! I'm so sorry.
Mother: You're sorry?

Two parents were waiting at the school gate. "Look at that teacher", said one to the other. "It's disgraceful. Jeans. An old T-shirt. Trainers. Cropped blue hair. You'd never think she was a teacher, would you?"

"Well I would actually. That's my child. We're meeting here to go shopping together."

"Oh I'm sorry. I didn't realize you were her mother."

"I'm not. I'm her father actually! And she's my son!"

At a very expensive school, the girls were discussing their family pets. "We have a beautiful spaniel at our place," said one girl.

"Does it have a pedigree?" asked another.

"It does on its mother's side. And its father comes from a very good neighborhood."

"What shall we play today?" said Theresa to her best friend Emma.

"Let's play schools," said Emma.

"OK!" said Theresa. "But I'm going to be absent."

At graduation day to mark the end of a particularly trying year, the principal said, "A parent said to me recently that half the teachers do all the work and the other half nothing at all. I'd like to assure all the parents here this afternoon that at this school the opposite is the case."

Why are American schoolchildren extremely healthy?
Because they have a good constitution.

At the school concert, Wee Willie had volunteered to play his bagpipes. The noise was dreadful, like a choir of cats singing off-key. After he'd blown his way through "The Flowers of the Forest" he said, "Is there anything you'd like me to play?"
"Yes!" cried a voice from the back of the hall. "Dominoes!"

What did the bookworm say to the school librarian?
Can I burrow this book please?

"And what might your name be?" the school secretary asked the new boy.
"Well, it might be Cornelius, but it's not. It's Sam."

What happened to the baby chicken that misbehaved in school?
It was eggspelled.

My dad is a real jerk. I told him I needed an encyclopedia for school and he said I'd have to walk just like everyone else!

My son's just received a scholarship to medical school – but they don't want him while he's alive.

Sandra's mother said no young man in his right mind would take her to the school dance in her bikini, so she decided to go with her friend's stupid brother.

Charlie: Our school is so old I don't know what stops it from falling down.

Edward: Maybe the woodworm hold hands.

Teacher: Where did Captain Cook land when he discovered Australia?
Sam: On his feet.

Why was Harold called the space cadet when he was in school?
Because he had a lot of space between his ears.

Did you hear about the schoolboy who was so lazy he went around with his mouth open to save him the trouble yawning?

What's the difference between a Popsicle and the school bully? You lick one, the other licks you.

Why was the cannibal expelled from school?
Because he kept buttering up the teacher.

What has eight feet and sings?
The school quartet.

What did the Eskimo schoolboy say to the Eskimo schoolgirl?
What's an ice girl like you doing in a place like this?

Knock, knock.
Who's there?
Ida.
Ida who?
Ida nawful time in school today.

Did you hear about the monster who went to night school to learn to read in the dark?

Father: Jennifer, I've had a letter from your principal. It seems you've been neglecting your appearance.

Jennifer: Dad?

Father: He says you haven't appeared in school all week.

Mother: What do you mean, the school must be haunted?

Daughter: Well, the principal kept going on about the school spirit.

Mother: What did you learn in school today?
Son: Not enough. I have to go back tomorrow.

Andy was late for school.
"Andy!" roared his mother. "Have you got your socks on yet?"
"Yes, Mom," replied Andy. "All except one."

First Middle-Aged Lady: I've kept my schoolgirl complexion.
Second Middle-Aged Lady: Yes, covered in spots.

Sid: Mom, all the boys in school call me Big Head.
Mom: Never mind, love, just pop down to the fruit and vegetable store and collect the 10 pounds of potatoes I ordered in your cap.

Mother: How was your first day in school?

Little Boy: OK, but I haven't got my present yet.

Mother: What do you mean?

Little Boy: Well the teacher gave me a chair, and said "Sit there for the present."

A little boy came home from his first day at kindergarten and said to his mother. "What's the use of going to school? I can't read, I can't write and the teacher won't let me talk."

Two little girls at a very posh school were talking to each other. "I told the chauffeur to take his peaked cap off in case the other girls here thought I was a snob," said the first.

"How strange," said the second. "I told mine to keep his on in case anyone thought he was my father."

Dinnertime

Some people say the school cook's cooking is out of this world.
Most pupils wish it was out of their stomachs.

Why are school cooks cruel?
Because they batter fish and beat eggs.

Teacher: Eat up your roast beef, it's full of iron.
Dottie: No wonder it's so tough.

Pupil to a dinner lady: Excuse me, but I have a complaint.
Dinner lady: This is the school dining room, not the doctor's office.

What did the dinner lady say when the teacher told her off for putting her finger in his soup?
It's all right, it isn't hot.

Brian: Our school must have very clean kitchens.
Bill: How can you tell?
Brian: All the food tastes of soap.

"I have decided to abolish all corporal punishment at this school," said the principal at morning assembly. "That means that there will be no physical punishment."
"Does that mean that you're stopping school dinners as well, Sir?"

Good news! At school today there will be free Coca-Cola for everyone . . . the bad news is that straws are 50 cents each!

Boy to Mother: Our school cook really knows her new technology as well as her history. For school dinner today we had micro-chips with ancient grease.

What do you get if you cross old potatoes with lumpy mince?
School dinners.

School meals are not generally popular with those that have to eat them, and sometimes with good reason. "What kind of pie do you call this?" asked one schoolboy indignantly.
"What's it taste of?" asked the cook.
"Glue!"
"Then it's apple pie – the plum pie tastes of soap."

"Any complaints?" asked the teacher during school dinner. "Yes, Sir," said one bold lad, "these peas are awfully hard, Sir." The master dipped a spoon into the peas on the boy's plate and tasted them. "They seem soft enough to me," he declared.
"Yes, they are now, I've been chewing them for the last half hour."

What's the difference between school dinners and a pile of slugs?
School dinners come on a plate.

A warning to any young sinner,
Be you fat or perhaps even thinner.
If you do not repent,
To Hell you'll be sent.
With nothing to eat but school dinner.

Why do vampires like school dinners?
Because they know they won't get stake.

A little demon came home from school one day and said to his mother, "I hate my sister's guts."
"All right," said his mother, "I won't put them in your sandwiches again."

I used to be thin.
Now I'm thinner.
So would you be.
With our school dinner.

Teacher to Dinner Lady: A pork chop, please and make it lean.
Dinner Lady: Certainly, Mr Smith, which way?

What's the difference between school dinners and a bucket of fresh manure?
School dinners are usually cold.

I smother school dinner with lots of honey.
I've done it all my life.
It makes the food taste funny.
But the peas stay on my knife.

Two girls were having their packed lunch in the schoolyard. One had an apple and the other said, "Watch out for worms won't you!" The first one replied "Why should I? They can watch out for themselves."

Darren, at school dinner: I've just swallowed a bone.
Teacher: Are you choking?
Darren: No, I'm serious.

How can you save school dumplings from drowning?
Put them in gravy boats.

Why did Rupert eat six school dinners?
He wanted to be a big success.

How can you tell when it's rabbit pie for school dinner?
It has hares in it.

Angry Teacher: I thought I told you to stand at the end of the canteen line!
Kevin: I did, Sir, but there was someone there already!

Teacher: If you eat any more, Ronald, you'll burst!
Ronald: Then you'd better stand clear, Sir, as I've just had a second helping!

Tracey: I've got cheese with holes in my sandwiches. I don't like cheese with holes in.
Stacey: Then eat the cheese and leave the holes at the side of your plate.

Where's the best place in school to have the sickroom?
Next to the canteen.

Mick: Why have you got a sausage stuck behind your ear?
Dick: What? Oh dear, I must have eaten my pencil at lunchtime.

Ted: Why do you call this Enthusiasm Curry?
Ned: Because the cook's put everything she's got into it.

Fussy Flora: Excuse me, but this egg tastes peculiar.
Dinner Lady: Don't blame me, I only laid the table.

Jez: This food isn't fit for a pig to eat!

Josh: I'll see if they've got any that is.

Will and Gill were comparing school meals with their mother's cooking.

"My mom's not that good a cook," said Gill, "but at least her gravy moves around on the plate."

Exams and Reports

Mother: Did you get a good place in the geography test?
Daughter: Yes, Mom, I sat next to the smartest kid in the class.

What do you have to take to become a medical examiner?
A stiff exam.

How do Religious Education teachers mark exams?
With spirit levels.

The night school teacher asked one of his pupils when he had last sat an exam. "1945," said the student.
"Good lord! That's more than fifty years ago."
"No, Sir! An hour and half, it's quarter after nine now."

Jennifer: How come you did so badly in history? I thought you had all the dates written on your sleeve?
Miriam: That's the trouble, I put on my geography blouse by mistake.

What kind of tests do they give in witch school?
Hex-aminations.

Why did the skeleton schoolgirl stay late at school?
She was boning up for her exams.

Why did the flea fail his exams?
He wasn't up to scratch.

A teacher was correcting exam papers when he came across Alec's effort: a sheet of paper, blank apart from his name and "'Macbeth,' Act Two, Scene Five, Line 28" The teacher reached for his Shakespeare and turned to "Macbeth" where he found that the 28th line of the fifth scene of the second act read, "I cannot do this bloody thing."

How did dinosaurs pass exams? With extinction.

When doing exams Dick knows all the answers. It's the questions that get him confused.

What's black and white and horrible?
A math examination paper.

Tommy was saying his prayers as his father passed by his bedroom door. "God bless Mommy, and God bless Daddy, and please make Calais the capital of France."

"Tommy," said his father, "why do you want Calais to be the capital of France?"

"Because that's what I wrote in my geography test!"

Which animals do you have to beware of when you take exams?

Cheetahs.

Pupil: Excuse me, Sir, but I don't think I deserve a mark of 0 for this exam paper.
Teacher: Neither do I, but it's the lowest mark I can give.

Knock, knock.
Who's there?
Sacha.
Sacha who?
Sacha lot of questions in this exam!

Which capital city cheats at exams?
Peking.

Teacher: In this exam you will be allowed ten minutes for each question.
Boy: How long is the answer?

When my dad finally passed his eleven-plus exam he was so excited he cut himself shaving.

"Alec," groaned his father when he saw his son's school report. "Why are you so awful at geography?"

"It's the teacher's fault, Dad. He keeps telling us about places I've never heard of."

Alec gave his father his school report one night. Dad was pleased to read that Alec's handwriting had improved tremendously. "But sadly," wrote the English teacher, "the improvement in the legibility of Alec's handwriting has revealed a great deficiency in his spelling."

Father: I see from your report that you're not doing so well in history. Why's this?

Son: I can't help it. He keeps asking me about things that happened before I was born.

"What's all this about?" roared Joan's dad, reading her school report. "Your teacher says he finds it impossible to teach you anything."

"I told you he was no good," said Joan.

What's the definition of a school report?
A poison pen letter from the principal.

It says on my report card that I tell lies – but it's not true.

Teacher: I hope I didn't see you cheating, Aggie.
Aggie: I hope you didn't, too, Miss.

Harry: I've just saved you $10, Dad.
Dad: How come?
Harry: You remember you said you'd give me $10 if I passed my exams?
Dad: Yes.
Harry: Well I didn't.

Mother: Why are you spanking Frankie?
Father: Because his exam results are due out tomorrow and I'll be away on business all day.

Teacher: You're always bottom of the class in exams, Otto. When are you going to get ahead?
Otto: I've already got one, Sir.

Which girl is very good at exams?
Anne Sirs.

When Angela had to write down on her exam paper the name of a liquid that won't freeze, she wrote "hot water."

Three friends were walking home from school one sunny afternoon. "What shall we do?" asked one. "Let's toss a coin," said another. "If it comes down heads, we'll go and play football, and if it comes down tails, we'll go for a swim in the river."

"Good idea," said a third. "And if it lands on its edge we'll go home and study for our exams."

School's Out

Barry: Who was that I saw you with last night?
Larry: It was a girl from the school.
Barry: Teacher?
Larry: Didn't have to!

Alex's class went on a nature study ramble. "What do you call a thing with ten legs, red spots and great big jaws, Sir?" asked Alex.
"I've no idea, why do you ask?" replied the teacher.
"Because one just crawled up your trouser leg."

"Dad," said Billy to his father who was a bank robber, "I need $50 for the school trip tomorrow."
"OK, son," said his dad, "I'll get you the cash when the bank closes."

Mary's class was taken to the Natural History Museum in London. "Did you enjoy yourself?" asked her mother when she got home.
"Oh yes," replied Mary. "But it was funny going to a dead zoo."

Mother: Did you enjoy the school outing, dear?
Jane: Yes. And we're going again tomorrow.
Mother: Really? Why's that?
Jane: To try and find the kids we left behind.

A teacher took her class for a walk in the country, and Susie found a snake. "Come quickly, Miss," she called, "here's a tail without a body!"

The class went to a concert. After, Jacqui asked the music teacher why members of the orchestra kept looking at a book while they played. "Those books are the score," replied the teacher. "Really?" replied Jacqui, "who was winning?"

How do insects travel when they go on vacation?
They go for a buggy ride.

At Christmas the school went to a special service in church. The teacher asked if they had enjoyed it, and if they had behaved themselves. "Oh yes, Miss," said Brenda. "A lady came round and offered us a plateful of money, but we all said no thank you."

What do you call a mosquito on vacation?
An itch-hiker.

"Why did you come back early from your vacation?" one of Alec's classmates asked him.

"Well, on the first day we were there one of the chickens died and that night we had chicken soup. The next day one of the pigs died and we had pork chops . . ."

"But why did you come back?"

"Well, on the third day the farmer's father-in-law died. What would you have done?"

Where do ghosts go on vacation?

The Dead Sea.

The class was taken to vist the opera, and afterwards young Daniel was asked if he had enjoyed it.

"Oh, yes," he replied. "But why did that man with a stick keep hitting that lady?"

"He wasn't hitting her, he was conducting the orchestra," said his teacher.

"But if he wasn't hitting her, why was she screaming?" asked Daniel.

What do demons have on vacation?
A devil of a time.

Did you hear what Dumb Donald did when he offered to paint the garage for his dad in the summer vacation? The instructions said put on three coats, so he went in and put on his blazer, his raincoat and his duffle coat.

Harry was telling his classmate about his vacation in Switzerland. His friend had never been to Switzerland, and asked, "What did you think of the scenery?"

"Oh, I couldn't see much," Harry admitted. "There were all those mountains in the way."

How do toads travel?

By hoppercraft.

My teacher is so stupid she thinks that aroma is someone who travels a lot.

Teacher: Now, remember, children, travel is very good for you. It broadens the mind.
Sarah, muttering: If you're anything to go by, that's not all it broadens!

Where do ants go on vacation?
Fr-ants

The pupils in the twelfth grade, who had learned to type, were being interviewed by prospective employers. Lisa was asked her typing speed. "I'm not sure," she replied. "But I can rub out at fifty words a minute."

"You never get anything right," complained the teacher. "What kind of job do you think you'll get when you leave school?"

"Well, I want to be the weather girl on TV."

Suresh: Whatever will Clive do when he leaves school? I can't see him being bright enough to get a job.
Sandra: He could always be a ventriloquist's dummy.

When you leave school, you should become a bone specialist. You've certainly got the head for it.

Sarah: Did you hear about Samantha now she's left school? She's working for a company that makes blotting paper.
Selina: Does she enjoy it?
Sarah: I believe she finds it very absorbing.

When I was in school I was as smart as the next fellow. What a pity the next fellow was such an idiot.